THE PONY EXPRESS

A HISTORY JUST FOR KIDS!

SAM ROGERS

KidLit-O Books
ANAHEIM, CALIFORNIA

Copyright © 2019 by Golgotha Press, Inc.

All rights reserved. No part of this publication may be reproduced, distributed or transmitted in any form or by any means, including photocopying, recording, or other electronic or mechanical methods, without the prior written permission of the publisher, except in the case of brief quotations embodied in critical reviews and certain other noncommercial uses permitted by copyright law.

Contents

About KidLit-O *1*

Introduction *3*

What Led Up to the Pony Express? *9*

Why Did the Pony Express happen? *15*

What Happened During the Days of the Pony Express? *21*

What Was It Like to Be a Kid During the Pony Express? *39*

How Did the Pony Express end? *44*

What Happened After the Pony Express? *51*

Conclusion *59*

ABOUT KIDLIT-O

KidLit-O is an imprint of BookCaps™ that is just for Kids! Each month BookCaps will be releasing several books in this exciting imprint. Visit bookcaps.com to learn more.

2 | The Pony Express

A rider for the Pony Express races to the next stop on his route. 1

---

1 Image source: http://historyofourmail.blogspot.com/p/pony-express.html

Introduction

Billy squinted his eyes a little in order to be able to see the road ahead in the darkness. His horse was galloping at a steady pace, and Billy himself felt pretty good. He had mounted the horse a few miles back, but something in the air wasn't quite right. There was no moon out, and some low clouds were covering the stars completely. Both Billy and the horse knew the way to the next station well enough, so he wasn't worried about getting lost or anything. But, as he rode along the path he knew so well, Billy was sure of one thing: he wasn't alone.

Even his horse was acting a little strangely, like it was afraid of something. The air was crisp here in Nevada, and the only sounds he could hear were the hoof beats of his steed. He had heard that this part of the route was dangerous, and that the local Native American tribe, the Paiute people, had just come out of a particularly difficult winter. Settlers in the area had been competing with the Paiute people for land and for natural resources. After a tough winter and an almost constant lack of food, the Paiute people had teamed up with two other tribes that lived nearby to wage war on the United States of America and on all of its citizens. Settlers and soldiers were all part of the war, in their eyes, but there was one group of people that represented everything they hated about the American way of doing things: the riders of the Pony Express.

Billy knew that, as he rode through the chilly Nevada night in May of 1860, any Paiute warriors who were watching the roads would be sure to hear him coming and would view it as a special privilege to kill him. After all, the riders of the Pony Express weren't easy targets.

Pulling his revolver from his holster, Billy leaned down closer to his horse to make himself a smaller target. The Native Americans might not respect him, but they respected his horse and knew how valuable it was. They would shoot their arrows high to avoid hitting it. Billy just hoped that luck was with him tonight.

As he rode towards the next stop on his route, about halfway before he could change places with another rider and get some sleep before riding back in the opposite direction, he heard some movement in the bushes beside him. Without waiting to see what it was, he yelled at his horse and nudged his spurs into its side. The horse ran faster than a minnow can swim a dipper, but, for a few moments, it looked like it might not be fast enough. Three Paiute braves came out into the road behind him, each one pulling an arrow back on his bow. He ducked as two arrows went flying over his head, and he said a silent prayer. It wasn't long before the danger was behind him. A few miles down the road, he honked the horn he carried with him to alert the attendant to prepare another horse.

Once he arrived, Billy jumped off his horse and turned back around to lift off the mochila, or mail bag, that he had been sitting on. By the light of the oil lamp burning near the stable, Billy could see something sticking out of the thick leather. An arrow. He pulled it out and threw it onto the ground. He had no time to worry about that now: he had to be back on the road in less than a minute, and the next horse was already waiting for him.

With his mochila over his shoulder, Billy jogged to the next horse and got ready for the next stage of his ride. Smiling to himself, he stepped into the stirrup and swung his thin frame over the horse and into the saddle. Without a word, he left the station attendant behind and raced into the night. His life was an adventure, and, arrows or no arrows, he loved every minute of it.

Have you ever heard of the Pony Express before? Do you know why young men like Billy were willing to risk their lives and ride in the dead of night to deliver mail? Do you know if anyone famous was ever part of the Pony Express?

In this handbook, we are going to learn all about this famous mail carrying service. We will see what it was like to ride the long trail from St. Joseph, Missouri to Sacramento, California alongside the Pony Express. What exciting things can you expect to learn?

First, we will learn what led up to the Pony Express. For example, how did so many people end up living in California during the mid-1800s? What were the other options for sending letters and small packages? Then, in the next section, we will see why the Pony Express was so necessary, and why it provided a service that no one else could at the time. We will see why whoever supplied the communication lines could make a difference in history.

The next section will be tremendously exciting as we will see how the Pony Express was started and what some of the biggest challenges were. Did you know that the Pony Express looked to hire young men who were orphans? Do you know why? We will find out. We will see the route that they travelled and see why these riders had to be fearless to do their job. Then, the next section will give you a chance to see what it was like to be a kid back then. You will climb into the saddle and ride along with the Pony Express over mountains and across rivers to get the mail to its destination on time.

After that, we will see a little more about how the Pony Express ended. Even though it was a particularly special arrangement, the world changed quickly and soon no one needed the Pony Express anymore. Then, we will find out what happened after.

Are you ready to start learning? Then grab your hat and let's go ride on the Pony Express!

[1]
WHAT LED UP TO THE PONY EXPRESS?

Prospectors in Northern California look for gold.[2]

The Pony Express was established as a rapid courier service between the East and the West, from St. Joseph Missouri to Sacramento, California. There were tens of thousands of people living and working in California that wanted

---

[2] Image source: http://www.goldrush.com/~joann/

news of what was happening in the East and who wanted to send letters and packages to friends, family members, and business partners living back east. But you may wonder: why did all those people move so far away from their friends and families back east in the first place? Why were they in California? Let's learn the answers.

As you may know, California did not always belong to the United States. Although different countries looked at owning a piece of the Pacific Coast for a long time, it was Spain who actually was the first to build permanent settlements as far north as the San Francisco Bay. The Spanish remained in control of California until 1821, when the local residents (the Mexican people) rebelled against Spain and gained their independence.

The land then came under Mexican control until 1846. During that time, more and more American settlers began to arrive and to raise crops, graze their livestock, and establish trading routes with the East. The settlers stayed mainly in the north while the Spanish-speaking

Mexican citizens (called Californios) stayed in the south. Although the two groups didn't actually like each other, California was large enough so that there was plenty of space between them and there weren't any serious problems. However, all of that changed on May 13, 1846, when the United States declared war on Mexico. After admitting Texas to the Union, a dispute with Mexico over the exact border between Texas and Mexico led to fighting among soldiers and eventually to a large war. The war ended on February 2, 1848, when the Treaty of Guadalupe Hidalgo was signed to end the war, and many lands, including California, were given to the United States.

Small groups of settlers started to move west, but in January of 1848, that small trickle of people going to California turned into a raging river when gold was discovered. Within a short time, some 300,000 people had moved to California to seek riches, and a lot of them were successful. Whole towns were built almost overnight, but people who moved to California didn't want to lose touch with the ones they behind. As a result, they were desperate to have communication with the outside world.

There were several ways of getting communication to the people living in the west, but none of them were fast, and they weren't always reliable. For example, some people sent their mail and packages by stagecoach. Do you know what a stagecoach is? Look at the picture below.

A stagecoach carried passengers and cargo in the Old West.3

3Image source: http://jamesanderson.authorsxpress.com/2012/07/16/in-which-class-do-you-travel/

Stagecoaches (like the one in the picture) went all over the Old West, carrying precious packages and letters to those who wanted them. However, do you know what the biggest problem with stagecoaches was? It could take around 24 days for the letter to reach its destination! And that wasn't even the worst of it. If someone were to send a letter or package by boat, it could have taken over a month! Think of waiting one month for a letter, for a reply to an important question, or to hear news.

If that seems almost unbelievable, think about the Mexican-American War that we mentioned earlier, the one that ended with the signing of the Treaty of Guadalupe Hidalgo. Even though war against Mexico was declared on May 13, 1846, the people living in California didn't find out officially for two months! Can you imagine that? The country was at war with California's next-door neighbor, but they didn't even know it!

As more and more people moved to the West, the need to have fast and reliable communication with the East became more critical than ever. The railroad still had a long way to go before it reached the Pacific Coast, and telegraph lines hadn't yet been approved for construction. Whoever could find a way to help people on opposite sides of the country communicate quickly with each other would become rich and famous and would help a lot of people along the way.

In 1860, three men came up with the perfect solution to the communication problem.

[2]
WHY DID THE PONY EXPRESS HAPPEN?

How relevant is communication in your life? Take a moment to think about how many people you communicate with every day. Be sure to include conversations, notes, text messages, phone calls, emails, and even status updates, tweets, and posts on social networks. Do you think you communicate with five people a day? Ten? Thirty? Fifty? More? Communication is important to all of us because it lets us be a part of the lives of the people we love, of our friends and families. Communication also lets us know what's happening around the world and lets us run our businesses. Now, imagine if you had to wait days or weeks to get a response to each message you sent out? How would you feel?

Back in the Old West, before there were telephone and telegraph lines put up everywhere, people had to wait weeks or even months for news to travel from one side of the country to the other. You can imagine how excited they were to get a letter or a note from someone they loved. However, communication with the West (and with California especially) became much more influential than simply sending letters or notes- it had to do with the future of the United States.

When California was accepted as a free state into the Union during the Great Compromise of 1850, the goal was to ease the growing tensions between the slave states and the non-slave states. For a time, there was even some talk of dividing California into two states, Northern and Southern, but that never happened. After California became a state in 1850, it became an indispensable place that both the Confederate States and the Union wanted on their side if a war were to break out.

What made California so desirable to both sides, especially taking into consideration the nearness of Civil War? Let's find out.

First, there was the issue of politics. There could be no doubt that a Civil War was coming- everybody could feel it in the air. The question was: which state would be on which side? Even though California has joined the Union as a free state, there was nothing stopping the people living there from changing their minds later and joining the Southern cause. In fact, there was even a pretty good-sized group of people living in California that wanted to have slavery and support the Confederates! As a result of such politics, there was a lot of interest in establishing and maintaining good communication with the West.

Another reason that so many people were interested in communicating with California and the West had to do with the gold that was being mined there. Whoever had California as a friend could be sure that they would get lots of financial help before, during, and after a war. And gold didn't just mean wealth- it meant power and having the best and latest technology. Later on, we will see what this all meant for the side who finally got to be friend with California.

Finally, everyone looked at the large population of the West. With some many tens of thousands of people who had moved there, each one of those people represented a vote that could either help or hurt the people in Washington. They represented potential soldiers for an army, workers in new industries, and business leaders to help the national economy. Communication with those people would ensure the strength of the entire nation and would make them a powerful friend to either the North or the South during the future Civil War.

Thus, to make sure that California would be friendly to their cause, one side or the other would have to promote regular communication with the people in charge there, including the politicians and the businessmen. Communication with the Old West became more valuable than simply sending letters back and forth; it became a fight for the very future of the United States. But what could the solution be? Stagecoaches took too long and had problems from hostile Native Americans and robbers along the way and boats took even longer.

Stagecoaches were often robbed while travelling in the Old west.4

Telegraph lines had been put up in key routes in the Eastern United States, but they only went as far west as St. Joseph, and no one from the government had offered money to put them even further west yet. In the meantime, a war was about to happen, and everyone

---

4 Image source: http://wedighistory.blogspot.com/2010/06/oregons-legends-of-lost-treasure.html

wanted California to be on their side. Who could come up with a solution to this difficult problem?

[3]
WHAT HAPPENED DURING THE DAYS OF THE PONY EXPRESS?

William H. Russell, William B. Waddle and Alexander Majors were the three founders of the Pony Express.5

Three American businessmen loyal to the Union saw a significant opportunity when they

---

5 Image source: http://www.xphomestation.com/

looked at the communication situation between the eastern United States and the West. These men, William H. Russell, William B. Waddle and Alexander Majors were already involved in the shipping business, working primarily with stagecoaches. However, they saw an opportunity to fill a gap in the communication systems that existed back then. They thought that they could find a faster way of transporting letters and small packages from the East to the West. If they were successful, they could help people stay in touch with loved ones, help tie California to the Union, and they could also get rich. What was their plan? They would use small horses and devoted riders as a fast delivery system.

What would the advantages be of using horses and riders instead of a stagecoach? Stagecoaches weighed more because they carried passengers and cargo. Sometimes, stagecoaches got stuck in the mud and the sand, and it took time to get them out. The horses got tired and needed to rest, and the roads weren't so great for the large wagons. However, one man riding on a horse could travel at about twice the speed of a stagecoach without the need to take frequent rests. However, the distance from St. Joseph to Sacramento was about 1,900 miles. No horse could ride that far without getting tired, and no rider could either. So, then, what was the solution?

The solution would be to have a series of horse stables built along the route about every ten miles or so. Each horse would travel at a moderately-paced gallop (about 10-15 miles per hour) for one "stage" of ten miles. As the rider got near the next stable, called a station-house, he would honk his horn or yell to let the attendant know that he needed to get another horse ready. When the rider arrived, another well-rested horse would be there to greet him. All he would have to do would be to throw his little mailbag into the saddle and take off again, letting the previous horse rest for a while. He would do this for about eight to ten hours, and cover between 75 and 100 miles. Then, another rider would take his mail bag and a fresh horse and keep riding. The tired rider would rest at the stationhouse for about eight hours before waking up to ride with some more mail back in the opposite direction, back where he came from.

The idea was genius! After all, instead of having to wait three or four weeks to get their mail and pertinent letters from St. Joseph, people in the West could now get what they needed in only nine or ten days! Can you understand why so many people got excited when they heard about the Pony Express? But now that the three men had the brilliant idea for the Pony Express, how would they make it happen? It took a lot of money and a lot of planning. They had to make a route, buy some horses, hire some riders, and then get some customers. Let's look at each of these things to see how the Pony Express dream became a reality.

Making the route. The first step towards establishing the Pony Express was deciding what route it would take. The most crucial decision was to decide what two cities would be on either end of the trail. The cities would have to be large and full of people who wanted to send correspondence to the other side of the country. The town of St. Joseph, Missouri was on the furthest western border of the state and would reduce the riding time instead of leaving from St. Louis or Kansas City.

St. Joseph had a telegraph line and could receive urgent message from cities like Boston, New York City, and Washington D.C. The messages could be quickly written down and carried by Pony Express to the intended recipient in a matter of days.

However, which city should be the one on the other side of the trail? Although most of the businessmen and people who wanted to use the service lived in San Francisco and Oakland, it was decided that Sacramento would be the city that the riders took the mail to. Why was Sacramento chosen? Well, from Sacramento, there were large boats (called ferries) that could take the mail the rest of the way to the Bay area (where San Francisco and Oakland were). That way, the new mail could be picked up, and the riders could start their journey eastward again.

So the two principal cities had been chosen: St. Joseph, Missouri on the eastern end and Sacramento, California on the Western end. A distance of some 1,900 miles separated the two cities. Which would be the best way to cross the plains and the mountains to get there? It was decided to follow the Oregon Trail west as far as Wyoming Territory. From there, the riders would head southwest across Utah and the Nevada Desert, climb over the Sierra Nevada Mountains, before heading across the California Central Valley to Sacramento.

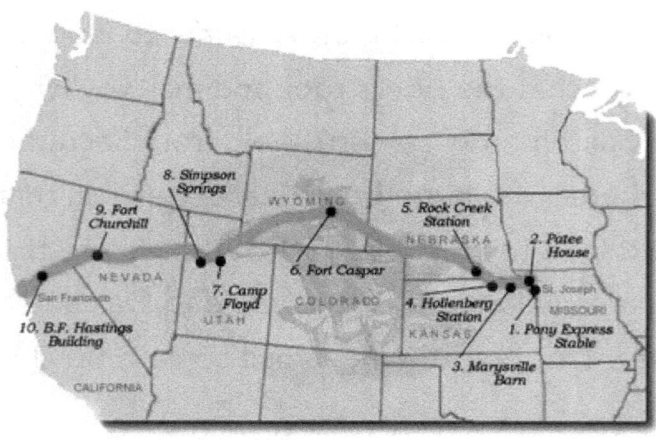

Can you see the route taken by the riders of the Pony Express?[6]

The route had been set. Now, they needed horses.

Buying the horses. What kind of horses do you think were bought for this new communication system? Remember the name "Pony Express". A "pony" refers to smaller horses that can run faster over longer distances. In fact, the majority of the horses bought for the Pony Express were only about 4 feet 10 inches tall, weighing about 900 pounds. (For a comparison, the average horse is about 5 feet 6 inches tall and weighs 1,200 pounds).

About 400 horses were bought from all over the West, most for $200 each. There were divided up into groups who lived and were cared for at 184 stations laid out along the Pony Express trail. The horses were well fed and were never worked too hard. They were rested after

---

[6] Image source: http://historyofourmail.blogspot.com/p/pony-express.html

running ten miles when the rider switched to a new horse.

Here, you can see Frank E. Webner, a Pony Express rider, and his horse in this 1861 picture.7

---

7 Image source: http://commons.wikimedia.org/wiki/File:Pony_-express.jpg

Now they had the trail and the horses, now they needed the riders. How would they get them?

Hiring the riders. If you were looking for someone to ride a horse along the route of the Pony Express, what kind of a person would you look for? Would his size matter? Would his age matter? What about his family? Have a look at an actual ad made by the Pony Express when they were looking for riders:

This is an actual poster printed by the Pony Express Company to find new riders.8

Did you see what kind of people the poster says they were looking for? It mentions young, skinny men. In fact, history tells us that none of the riders on the Pony Express weighed more than 110 pounds. Why do you think they wanted men who didn't weight too much? Well, think about this: horses can only carry a certain amount of weight before they tire out and even get injuries. So that means that if the rider weighs less, then the horse can carry more mail, and the company (who charges for the weight of each letter) would make more money. Also, a lighter load meant that the horse would run faster and get the mail to its destination sooner.

Orphans were preferred because of the long distance that the riders would travel. Even though most of the riders weren't orphans, the idea was to have riders who wouldn't be too

---

8 Image source: http://mommamindyprairieprimer.wordpress.com/category/pony-express/

worried thinking about leaving behind their families. They wanted serious men who would focus on the job. Also, the poster said: "Must… be willing to risk death daily." As you can imagine, a job like that attracted a certain type of person: somebody who was looking for adventure.

One of the founders of the Pony Express, Alexander Majors, was a religious man and asked each of the new riders to take a special oath:

> "I _____ do hereby swear, before the great and living God, that during my engagement, and while I am an employee of Russell, Majors, & Waddell, I will, under no circumstances, use profane language. I will drink no intoxicating liquors; that I will not quarrel or fight with any other employee of the firm, and that in every respect, I will conduct myself honestly, faithful to my duties, and so direct my acts as to win the con-

fidence of my employers. So help me God."[9]

This oath helped the new riders to understand that they were about to start something dead serious. The young men were to act as gentlemen even when riding through the Wild West. Instead of being just another cowboy, they were to represent the best that the American culture had to offer.

What did a pony express rider take with him on his rides? The single most indispensable item was the mochila, or mailbag, as seen in the picture below.

---

[9] Quotation source: http://www.blm.gov/ut/st/en/fo/salt_lake/recreation/back_country_byways/pony_express_trail/story_of_the_pony.html

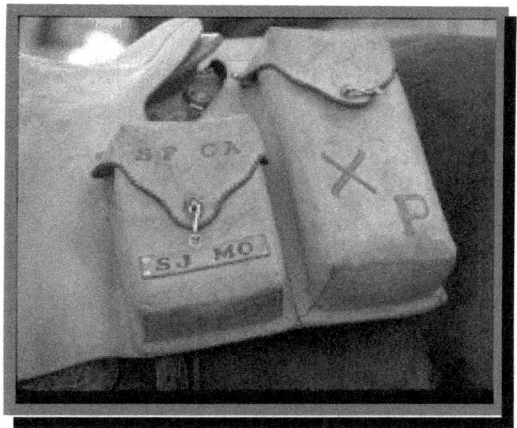

A "mochila" or mailbag was used by riders on the Pony Express.10

Inside the mochila, up to about 20 pounds worth of mail could be carried. The rider would also take a canteen of water with him, a bible, a revolver for personal protection, and a horn for letting the station attendants know when he was arriving (although many later riders stopped carrying a horn).

Each rider made $25 per week. Was that a lot of money back then? Well, for comparison, the average laborer made only about $1 per

---

10 Image source: http://historyofourmail.blogspot.com/p/pony-express.html

week, so you can imagine how happy the riders were every time payday came around!

Several famous cowboys from the Old West got their start riding for the Pony Express, including William Cody (better known as Buffalo Bill). Buffalo Bill was present for every major event in the Old West and Frontier America, including the Gold Rush, the construction of the railroad, and even the Civil War. As a rider for the Pony Express, he once had to ride 322 miles nonstop during 21 hours, using 21 different horses to deliver the mail! Most of the riders were willing to work just as hard. Once the route had been chosen, and the horses and riders had been obtained, the Pony Express only had to find its customers and carry their mail. How did they do so?

Getting the customers. From the very beginning, the founders of the Pony Express knew that their business wouldn't last forever. But until the telegraph and railroad were completed, they knew that they could provide a valuable service for lots of people. Their first hope was to secure a contract with the U.S.

Government to be the exclusive (only) carrier of Federal and Army communications. However, when that didn't happen (the contract went to a stagecoach company) the founders decided to focus on private businessmen and wealthy citizens. The price of carrying letters wasn't cheap, so not everyone could afford it. However, to those who had the money and who needed an urgent response to something, the price was worth it. How much did the Pony Express charge for carrying letters across the country? Look at the following quote from one reference work:

> "The cost to send a 1/2 ounce letter was $5.00 at the beginning [and was] a costly sum in those days and mostly unaffordable to the general public. By the end period of the Pony Express, the price had dropped to $1.00 per 1/2 ounce. Even the $1.00 rate was considered a lot of money ($26 in 2012 U.S. Dollars)."[11]

---

[11] Quotation source: http://en.wikipedia.org/wiki/Pony_Express

As you can see, not everyone could use the Pony Express, mainly just the government and rich businesspeople. However, the Pony Express earned a good reputation and only ever lost one mailbag (after an attack by Paiute Native Americans in 1860). How did the Pony Express advertise their services? They got new clients by putting up posters everywhere similar to the one below.

This is an actual poster used to tell people about the new Pony Express rapid mail delivery company.12

Within a short time, people wanted to see just how good this service was. On April 3, 1860, they got their chance. Look at the following description of what the first ride was like:

"On April 3, 1860, the first official delivery began at the eastern terminus of the Pony Express in St. Joseph, Missouri. Amid great fanfare and with many dignitaries present, a mail pouch containing 49 letters, five telegrams and miscellaneous papers was handed to a rider. At 7:15 p.m., a cannon was fired and the rider bolted off to a waiting ferry boat.

The Pony Express was set up to provide a fresh horse every 10-15 miles and a fresh rider every 75-100 miles. 75 horses were needed to-

---

12 Image source: http://en.wikipedia.org/wiki/File:Pony_Express_Poster.jpg

tal to make a one-way trip. Average speed was 10 miles per hour. On April 9 at 6:45 p.m., the first rider from the east reached Salt Lake City, Utah. Then, on April 12, the mail pouch reached Carson City, Nevada at 2:30 p.m.

The riders raced over the Sierra Nevada Mountains, through Placerville, California and on to Sacramento. Around midnight on April 14, 1860, the first mail pouch was delivered via the Pony Express to San Francisco."[13]

Can you imagine how exciting it must have been to see the riders leave, to watch them race across the country, and then finally arrive in Sacramento?

The Pony Express dream had become a reality, and everyone was tremendously excited about it.

---

[13] Quotation source: http://www.nps.gov/poex/historyculture/history1.htm

[4]
WHAT WAS IT LIKE TO BE A KID DURING THE PONY EXPRESS?

Can you imagine riding alongside someone like Buffalo Bill as he raced through the Great Plains, the Nevada desert, or over the Sierra Nevada mountains? Can you imagine looking out for hostile Native Americans and trying to ride faster than robbers chasing you? Do you see the surprised looks on the faces of the stagecoach drivers as you go racing past them and leaving them to eat your dust? That would have been a lot of fun!

There is no doubt about it: the riders on the Pony Express led lives of adventure. They were awake and riding at night when the whole world was fast asleep. They rode through the rain, through the snow, and through the hottest days you can imagine. Their missions were so momentous that they didn't stop to speak to anyone on the way. All they thought about was: make it to the next station.

The riders were supposed to get a rest every eight hours or so, after changing horses seven or eight times. However, there were occasions, like the one we saw with Buffalo Bill, when the new riders weren't ready, were sick, or were missing. What would happen then? The young men would have to do the same thing that Buffalo Bill did: keep on riding. Even though they were tired, they would have to keep on riding all the through the next stage. The mail had to be delivered.

Was it always fun and adventure on the Pony Express trail? Unfortunately, things weren't always so enthusiastic. Even though the pay was good and the riders tried to get along with everyone they met, the country was going through some serious problems. Do you remember the problems that many settlers were having with the Paiute Native American tribe? Do you remember what the problem was about?

Try to see things from the perspective of the Paiute people. For generations, they had lived on their land and hunted and raised crops. They had borders with other Native American tribes in the area and their leaders tried terribly hard to keep the peace with everyone. However, as more and more Americans began to cross through their lands, to build houses and farms, and to settle it, they were forced to grow crops in smaller areas, share their hunting grounds with more people, and fight to defend the borders that had been established for so long.

The Paiute tribe, along with other tribes in the area, saw their way of life being threatened. They felt that the only way to stay alive and to stay together as a people was to fight against the settlers and to kill the people who they saw as taking away their land and their freedoms. The Pony Express, because it was always riding through Paiute territory and because it represented Americans expanding westward, became a distinct target. One young man, named, Billy Tate, was only 14 years old when he was killed by some Paiute Native American warriors. He killed seven of his attackers before dying himself. Note how one reference work explains his brave last fight:

> "14-year old Billy Tate is often cited as the bravest pony rider of them all. Delivering mail at the height of a war with the local Indian tribes in the Ruby Valley of Utah, Tate was often pursued, but was able to escape thanks to his horses being able to outrun Indian horses.
>
> Tate's luck finally ran out, when Indians ambushed and surrounded him. Tate fought to the death. Finally falling from his horse, Tate's last act was to grab the mailbag and shield it with his body. As a mark of respect for the young man's courage, the Indians reattached his mailbag to the saddle, marked it with a sign of inviolability, and let the mustang go. Several hours later, the horse arrived at the nearest

settlement alone, bringing the post but not its rider."14

Knowing that something so terrible happened to Billy Tate would have made anyone sad. But if you were a rider, would that have made you stop? Of course not; the riders of the Pony Express believed that they had a serious job to do, and they were determined to make sure the mail got to its destination, even if they had to ride hard, fast, and for a long time.

To have been a kid back then would have meant having a life of adventure!

---

14 Quotation source: http://sixthscaleamericanhistory.yuku.com/topic/1565#.ULd5F6xTxeA

[5]
HOW DID THE PONY EXPRESS END?

The Pony Express was an exciting idea, and we already saw the first successful ride on April 3, 1860. For nineteen months, the Pony Express ran twice weekly without any interruptions (with the exception of a few during the Paiute wars). After nineteen months, on October 26, 1861, the Pony Express announced its official closure. What had happened to close this exciting chapter of American history? There were at least three factors: unmet expectations, the telegraph, and the railroad. Let's look at each of them.

Unmet expectations: The Pony Express got people excited because they hoped to receive regular news reports from the East Coast. And while, in some special cases, this did indeed happen (like during the 1860 Presidential Election) in most cases the Pony Express focused on carrying personal communication between people. As a result, many of those living on the West Coast felt a little disappointed and just as cut off as always from current events back east. Also, the price stayed so high that those hoping to use the service could never actually afford it. It was just too expensive for an average person to use (anywhere from one weeks' to one months' worth of wages!)

The founders themselves were disappointed with the financial results of the Pony Express. They had spent about $200,000 to start the business and to keep it running, but only made back $90,000. The high expectations that the founders had for the Pony Express were never fully realized.

Let's look at another reason the Pony Express ended.

The Telegraph. Do you know what the telegraph was? The telegraph, invented in the United States by Samuel Morse and Alfred Vail, was a method of sending electrical signals over long distances. The code, called "Morse Code," would be translated into letters and words. A station on each side would either broadcast or receive the message, writing it down for the recipient. Although it was not as personal as a handwritten letter, the telegraph could transmit key messages instantly over long distances (it would be used during the Civil War to allow Lincoln to direct his troops with up-to-date information). But what did the telegraph have to do with the end of the Pony Express?

Remember, the Pony Express was not for everyday communication; it was only for urgent letters and news. When the telegraph finally reached all the way from the east coast to the west coast, those same fundamental messages could then be sent by telegraph. As a result, the Pony Express was not needed anymore.

This came as a surprise to no one, even to the founders of the Pony Express. However, they had hoped that, in the meantime, they would make more money along the way. The

First Transcontinental Telegraph was installed and connected on October 24, 1861, and the Pony Express closed its doors two days later.
The Railroad.

The completion of the Transcontinental Railroad is pictured here.15

On May 10, 1869, the Transcontinental Railroad, going from San Francisco, California, all the way to New York City on the East Coast was completed. Now, large steam trains carrying cargo, passengers, and correspondence

---

15 Image source: http://en.wikipedia.org/wiki/File:69workmen.jpg

could travel from one side of the country to the other quickly. How quickly?

While a ship would take several weeks to make the journey coast to coast (going around the tip of South America) and taking a wagon would have lasted several months, one train that left New York City on June 4, 1876 arrived in San Francisco just 83 hours and 39 minutes later. In other words, the people crossed the country in only about three and a half days! That is even faster than the Pony Express could ever have hoped to travel.

Even though the Pony Express was a terrific idea and it did its job exceedingly well for nineteen months, technology kept improving, and eventually the new technology could do things that the Pony Express riders and even stagecoaches never could. The train didn't have to worry about thieves, about Native American attacks, about horses getting tired, or even about too much rain. The train could run 24 hours a day, as long as there was enough fuel, and could carry thousands and thousands of pounds of letters, not just one bag full.

In the quickly changing United States, especially after the Civil War, urgent messages were sent by telegraph and letters and correspondence were sent by train. The world had changed, and the Pony Express had finished its job.

After the Civil War, the remaining horses and materials from the Pony Express were sold to Wells Fargo. Wells Fargo was a stagecoach company that served the little tows far away from the train stations that still needed stagecoaches to move people and goods around. However, even Wells Fargo would have to change their job as the trains and then roads and automobiles took over one piece of land after another. Today, the Wells Fargo company focuses on banking and no longer on express shipping.

Do you think that we should be sad about the end of the Pony Express? Well, it's understandable that when we see something as exciting as the Pony Express, we want it to last forever. However, it is essential to realize that even the founders of the company knew that it would only last for a little while. The important thing to realize is that all of those riders (there were eventually about 120 of them) worked hard to get a job done, and they earned the reputation as the bravest and most trustworthy mail carriers anywhere.

Even though the Pony Express only lasted about nineteen months, it played a hugely prominent role in American history and had lasting consequences as we will see in the next section.

[6]
WHAT HAPPENED AFTER THE PONY EXPRESS?

After the Pony Express ended, everyone who had been involved went their separate ways. Some of them kept trying to make new businesses, others kept looking for adventure. For example, Buffalo Bill became one of the most famous Americans in the world for having a travelling show that talked all about the Wild West and including horse tricks, shooting, and reenactments of famous battles.

However, the Pony Express had affected at least one particularly significant part of American history: the role of California in the Civil War. Do you remember that we spoke earlier about how influential California was to both sides in the Civil War? California, because of the Gold Rush, had a large population and a lot of money. The 1860 census found that there were 379,985 people living in California, larger than the population of such eastern states as Vermont, New Hampshire, Delaware, and even Florida. That large number gave California increased voting power in the House of Representatives. As a result, both the North and the South wanted California on their side. However, when war finally broke out, California supplied troops and money to the Union, not to the Confederacy. What was a key factor in keeping California loyal to the Union? It was the Pony Express.

The Pony Express let the Federal Government keep good communication with California and to convince the people there to remain a part of the Union. With no communication coming from the South, the Californians felt no loyalty there. As a result, lots of California gold was sent to Union soldiers to buy weapons, food, and even things as simple as shoes. The Confederate army, without the sale of its profitable cotton and without outside help, soon entered into rough times, sometimes marching into battle with bare feet and empty stomachs.

California, because of the communication provided by the Pony Express and the Union loyalty that came with it, also helped to fight any possible rebellion within its borders and even over in New Mexico. The Union had gained a powerful and faithful friend when California joined its side. President Lincoln, the President of the Union during the Civil War, later wrote about how much he appreciated all that California had done. He said:

"I have long desired to see California; the production of her gold mines has been a marvel to me, and her stand for the Union, her generous offerings to the Sanitary (Commission), and her loyal representatives have endeared your people to me; and nothing would give me more pleasure than a visit to the Pacific shore, and to say in person to your citizens, 'God bless you for your devotion to the Union,' but the unknown is before us. I may say, however, that I have it now in purpose when the railroad is finished, to visit your wonderful state."16

The Pony express, even though it lasted for such a short time, became an important part of the Old West, especially as we think about it today. Really, what symbol better sums up the tough conditions, the hard work ethic, and the danger that meant moving out west? Mark Twain, a famous American author, once wrote about the arrival of a Pony Express rider that he saw while travelling through the Old West. Have a look at how he describes the scene, in his book Roughing It:

> "In a little while all interest was taken up in stretching our necks and watching for the "pony-rider"—the fleet messenger who sped across the continent from St. Joe to Sacramento, carrying letters nineteen hundred miles in eight days! Think of that for perishable horse and human flesh and blood to do! The pony-rider was usually a little bit

---

16 Quotation source: http://www.parks.ca.gov/?page_id=26775

of a man, brimful of spirit and endurance. No matter what time of the day or night his watch came on, and no matter whether it was winter or summer, raining, snowing, hailing, or sleeting, or whether his "beat" was a level straight road or a crazy trail over mountain crags and precipices, or whether it led through peaceful regions or regions that swarmed with hostile Indians, he must be always ready to leap into the saddle and be off like the wind! There was no idling-time for a pony-rider on duty. He rode fifty miles without stopping, by daylight, moonlight, starlight, or through the blackness of darkness—just as it happened. He rode a splendid horse that was born for a racer and fed and lodged like a gentleman; kept him at his utmost speed for ten miles, and then, as he came crashing up to the station where stood two men holding fast a fresh, impatient steed, the transfer of rider and mail-bag was made in the twinkling of an eye, and away flew the eager pair and were out of sight before the spectator could get hardly the ghost of a look. Both rider and horse went "flying light." The rider's dress was thin, and fitted close; he wore a "round-about," and a skull-cap, and tucked his pantaloons into his boot-tops like a race-rider. He carried no arms—he carried nothing that was not necessary, for even the postage on his literary freight was worth five dollars a letter.

He got but little frivolous correspondence to carry—his bag had business letters in it, mostly. His horse was stripped of all unnecessary weight, too. He wore a little wafer of a racing-saddle, and no visible blanket. He wore light shoes, or none at all. The little flat mail-pockets strapped under the rider's thighs would each hold about the bulk of a child's primer. They held many and many an important business chapter and newspaper letter, but these were written on paper as airy and thin as gold-leaf, nearly, and thus bulk and weight were economized.

Every neck is stretched further, and every eye strained wider. Away across the endless dead level of the prairie a black speck appears against the sky, and it is plain that it moves. Well, I should think so!

In a second or two it becomes a horse and rider, rising and falling, rising and falling—sweeping toward us nearer and nearer—growing more and more distinct, more and more sharply defined—nearer and still nearer, and the flutter of the hoofs comes faintly to the ear—another instant a whoop and a hurrah from our upper deck, a wave of the rider's hand, but no reply, and man and horse burst past our excited faces, and go winging away like a belated fragment of a storm!

So sudden is it all, and so like a flash of unreal fancy, that but for the flake of white foam left quivering and perishing on a mail-sack after the vision had flashed by and disappeared, we might have doubted whether we had seen any actual horse and man at all, maybe."[17]

---

[17] Quotation source: http://www.gutenberg.org/files/3177/3177-h/3177-h.htm#linkch08

People loved the Pony Express, and down to this day when we think of the Wild West, we think of Cowboys, Native Americans, and the Pony Express.

Conclusion

We have learned a lot about the Pony Express. Let's have a brief review of the handbook.

First, we learned what led up to the Pony Express. For example, do you remember how so many people ended up living in California during the mid-1800s? It was because of the Gold Rush. Thousands and thousands of people moved to California to strike it rich, and many brought their families with them. All of these people, especially the businessmen and politicians wanted to send and receive letter from the East Coast. Do you remember what the other options for sending letters and small packages were? They could send packages by boat, but that could take up to a month. A stagecoach wasn't much better: it would take at least three or more weeks just to make it to Missouri.

Then, in the next section, we saw why the Pony Express was so necessary. As you will remember, communication was hugely important at that point in history because the Civil War was about to break out. Everyone wanted to California to be on their side, and people wanted to know what was happening on the other side of the country. Also, we saw how the Pony Express provided a service that no one else at the time could.

The section after that was exciting because we saw how the Pony Express was started and what some of the biggest challenges were. Remember, they had to build little stations along a 1,900 mile route and put about 400 horses along the way. Then, do you remember the kind of rider they were looking for? Like we learned, the Pony Express looked to hire young men who were orphans and paid them about $25 a week for their hard work. It was in that section that we saw the route that they travelled and see why these riders had to be fearless to do their job.

Then, the next section will gave us a chance to see what it was like to be a kid back then. We climbed into the saddle and rode along with the famous riders of the Pony Express (like Buffalo Bill) over mountains and across rivers to get the mail to its destination on time.

After that, we saw a little more about how the Pony Express ended. Even though it was a truly unique arrangement, the world changed mightily quickly and soon no one needed the Pony Express anymore. The two biggest changes were the telegraph and the railroad. The railroad could get people and letters from one coast of the country to the other even faster than the Pony Express could, and they never had to worry about tired horses.

Then, we found out what happened after. We saw how valuable California became in the Civil War, and how the legacy of the Pony Express rider lived on forever. Do you remember Mark Twain's exciting experience and how excited everyone was to see the Pony Express rider?

Even though we don't use telegraphs today, and most of us use cars, not trains, we should take some time to think about the Pony Express and the men who started it. Why should we care? The men who started and ran the Pony Express wanted to help people and to solve a problem that they saw. They used their own money, and they found people just as dedicated as they were to work hard and to get the job done. We have lots of problems today, and we need people who are willing to find good solutions and to take a risk to get the job done.

Although Buffalo Bill and Billy Tate died a long time ago, their legacy lives on. What do you think? Would you have been willing to ride on the Pony Express? Are you willing to do brave and difficult things today in order to get the job done? Be like the riders on the Pony Express, and never stop moving forward!